Elizabeth Jackson Barker

POEMS IN PASSAGE

North Country Books
Utica, New York
1988

First Printing 1988

Cover Design and Illustrations by Domingo Barreres

Library of Congress Cataloging-in-Publication Data
Barker, Elizabeth Jackson, 1911-
    Poems in passage/Elizabeth Jackson Barker.—1st ed.
        p.   cm.
    ISBN 0-932052-73-8 : $12.50.   ISBN 0-932052-72-X (pbk.) : $6.00
    I. Title.
    PS3552.A6167P64 1988
    811'.54—dc19   88-31149
                                                              CIP

Dedication

To the memory of Guy Barker

ACKNOWLEDGEMENTS

The author is indebted to George Starbuck and to the late
Samuel French Morse for their encouragement, their
criticism, and the inspiring example of their poems.

Poems Previously Published

"Yes and No Stories" *Virginia Quarterly Review*
(also in *Best Poems of 1959*. Pacific Books, Palo Alto, CA.)

"The Names of the Rose" *Virginia Quarterly Review*

"Nocturne: Lullaby for Laika" *Virginia Quarterly Review*
(The three above have won first in the Emily Clark Balch Prizes)

"Letter from Mrs. Hoshino" *Trinity Review* (Hartford, CT.)

"First Period" *Trinity Review* (Hartford, CT.)

"Block Island, Again" *Harvard Advocate* (Cambridge, MA.)

"Twenty Days, Twenty Years"
Harvard Advocate (Cambridge, MA.)

"A Point" *Harvard Advocate* (Cambridge, MA.)

"Grade Crossing, 1933" *Harvard Advocate* (Cambridge, MA.)

"Mabel: I Saw Her and It Was I" *Boston Review*

"After Perrault or, It's Not the Witch's Story" *Denver Quarterly*

"... questa selva selvaggia ..." *Denver Quarterly*

"I Give These Books for the Founding of a College in This Colony"
Denver Quarterly
(Reynolds Award, Poetry Society of America)

"Good Friday AM, Without Cock-Crow"
Ex Libris (Boston University, MA.)

"Art, Life, and a Hirschkafer" *Ex Libris* (Boston University, MA.)

"The Tradition Still Traduces" *Ex Libris* (Boston University, MA.)

CONTENTS

POEMS IN PASSAGE

"YES AND NO STORIES"

Always choices three and choosers losers:
The crossroads and the brothers' triple quest
To seize the horse whose hooves outstrike the hours,
Steal the heart's-ease nightingale, and quench
The dragon lately laying waste the fields
(The public-spirited princess as a prize).

They walk together to the tale's beginning,
Where three roads (never two) suggest they part.
(The grandfathers told it as they knew:
Choice is not convenient "this or that,"
But "this or what?" Three might be a hundred;
Hence the tripartition of the road.)

A forest lies ahead, but not a sign,
Not a sagging, weathered finger-post
Names a distant, unfamiliar town.
Their shoes already sopping in the dew,
A little awed by the ambiguous
Dimension of the dawn, the brothers choose
Which road for which, but only two decide.
The youngest waits for what is his, accepts,
As we accept, who know, content to wait
To watch the cunning choosers brought to naught:
Mispronounce the magic word, spit on
The ragged man who holds the castle's key,
And take the golden bridle, not the horse.
They walk among the cinders of the farms,
Nor ever guess the dragon is their guide;
Come bitter backward, looking at their feet;
Pass here, protesting they are not to blame.

The one who follows the unchosen road
Will hear a footfall in the forest; learn
The word that turns the lock, because he asks
A seedy fox with whom he feels no shame
To share a meal and time in conversation.
He takes the nightingale and leaves the cage;
Investigates the habits of the dragon,
His curiosity engaged the while
Before he slips a sword between the scales.
Sometime, recalling at this intersection
The face, intent and dubious in the dawn
Upon the fox's track that was his portion,
He smiles to recognize it as his own.

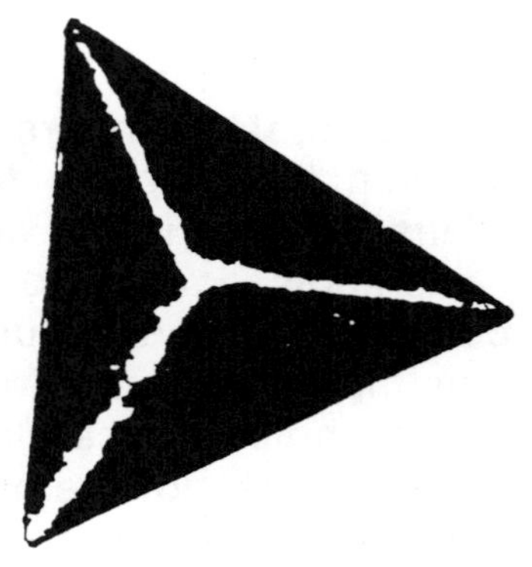

THE NAMES OF THE ROSE,
Or, What the Word Said

So stated, so it is, yet isn't so:
Children's wisdom, plausible, inane;
I was first to let you know you know.

Do you never smell me when the snow
Mounds the bush and lies along each cane?
So stated, so it is, yet isn't so.

When damp Creation waited in a row,
I was whispering in Adam's brain:
I was first to let you know you know.

And I am, last, all you will have to show:
A line engraved beneath a lichen stain.
So stated, so it is, yet isn't so.

I walk beside you where the whirlwinds blow,
That you may tell the slayer from the slain:
I was the first to let you know you know.

The gift ambiguous that I bestow
Is but a hand-me-down from Jubal-Cain:
So stated, so it is, yet isn't so;
I was the first to let you know, you know.

NOCTURNE
(Lullaby for Laika)

Cain with Thorns rose neither late nor soon
To witness, from the vantage of his arc,
The hurried cycle of a little moon,
Its month in minutes: dark, to full, to dark.
Unrisen Sirius, by Orion keeping
Faithful company time out of mind,
Heard the muffled barks above the beeping
And recognized another of his kind.
Informed of what we neither saw nor heard,
We wanted reassurance it was tame;
All day we memorized a foreign word
That night might seem familiar when it came.
   None, in comfort's pale of wind and fog,
    Would whistle home the Hunter's newest dog.

"I give these Books for
the founding of a
College in this Colony"
(to Daniel, Domingo, Sara, Rebekah)

I

For you I click the switches in the stacks
this undecided end-of-winter day:
the old lions in custom calf-skin backs
are shelved these shadowed aisles and years away
by number here. I light them with a pale
and naked globe and wonder, as we move,
if you will notice that the air is stale,
if you will scorn an unselective love.

II

Past palaces and gibbets flowed in song
the current burden of an old despair:
the golden Progress hardly lasts as long
as the voices hymning on the water-stair;
and they who found a haven in this town
left Lycidas and all those nymphs behind:
the window opens only out, and down,
so meanly it informs this storied mind.

III

A private round of living dog goes by
where troubled puddles hold, then break and flaw
the whole reflection of a clearing sky.
The wind is bound tonight to end the thaw
and seal our stream that never knew a swan:
we see but cannot hear it in this place;
we exercise our option to be gone.
An elevator drops us to such grace
as might illuminate an afternoon
where hoary ambiguities abound
outside the wickets of the opportune
(though there are only fishes in the Sound)

IV

Remaining minutes through the meter run
untended by the hand that set the glass
in mindless motion, mindfully begun.
Now we pull out beyond this curb and pass
the last night's papers sucked against a fence,
to join the stream where half New Haven rides
with thought of neither loss nor recompense
on avenues called after regicides.

A POINT

A holy man came out of his cave,
out of a flaw in a mountain of glass:
"Whatever is mine I shall break in half,"
he said, "for whoever may happen to pass.
For I'll beg the question to die or live
if fasting is nothing; but something to give,
I think, might argue a point for life."
He bought some grain and baked a loaf
and next day sat at his door like a spider,
waiting the wandering man who came
empty and open to any offer,
early abroad from a supperless dream.
The holy man held out his hand.
The other reached: a tongue of knife
licked the fingers that touched the bread.
With a cry the wanderer leaped and ran.
Then the holy man saw what that man had seen
and wondered which of them had bled.

MABEL: I SAW HER AND IT WAS I

She sat in Cincinnati, middle-aged,
neat, neutral bird, remarkable
chiefly in being unremarkable;
had nothing to commend her to the eye
or ear, yet occupied a private cage
with a placard on the wire requesting news
of others like her. Mother read aloud,
"Their flights once hid the sun . . . the sky
. . . A hundred dollars for a healthy male."
She bent and bit the feathers of her breast
removed, unmoved, amid a crowd
of tricky Chinese pheasants, cockatoos
like the jeweled caskets in a fairy tale
(step-sisters' choices, but I had liked them best)
I wondered where her relatives had gone;
I stared and rubbed my nose along the rail.
(This was in September, World War One
and I was wearing buttoned shoes.)

For the week or two we saw her daily
she stayed single.(We were moving then,
living in a house where a lady
couldn't bear to hear a sound,
in a room upstairs with nothing to do.
The porch was dark with trumpet vines and men
who didn't smell like anyone we knew,
and some pods on a catalpa tree hung down
like cut off hands outside our window.
(Mother took us every morning to the zoo.)

"Slaughtered and shipped by the barrel to the East":
silly birds, each annual migration
they packed their nests so close along the limbs
and tier on tier (to chat away the hatching time?)
a shot, a stone would bring a dozen down,
a storm wipe out a generation.
In Michigan one had. The farmers turned
their hogs into the woods to feast
on eggs and embryos and fledglings.
Remnant parents came each spring but never learned
to sacrifice their sociability,
nor even at the end inferred their ending.

I said I'd see what I could do. She poked
among her feathers, unconcerned.
Each day I said, "Just wait." I looked
among the trumpet vines along the porch
and in the ugly podded tree
and in the zoo. And then we moved. My search,
recalled from time to time, went on
in places foreign to her habitat,
till once in nineteen forty-three
I counted up the years and thought
how from the most protected perch
a bird might drop alone from age
one unimaginable morning.
Extinction can amount to that:
a female pigeon in a littered cage
—or is a species' exit different
from the routine sparrow accident?
I left off looking.

No one seems to know of this but me.
Ectopistes migratorius
is known, and the civilizing waste
that laid it low. But not this.
Did I make her up? Mother remembers
the zoo, the boarding house, September,
and World War One: but not the last
passenger pigeon sitting in the world spinster,
nor the gaslit nights when tumid catalpa
pods on their amputated boughs
were groping the bedroom wall, nor the dim veranda
of salesmen with their secret laughter
at the fledgling's fall, the hunger of the great sows.

MASS. PIKE

Sometimes a steeple
startles
the dull meeting edge
of earth and sky—
a place!
The roofs and chimneys over there
cluster, chances are,
around a name.
We need not know.
Eastbury, Westbury, the same
embankment holds us high
in the valley, cuts us low
in the hill.
The cultured grass blurs back
to where we hesitated last
and clears a sceneless track
to where we go.
Going is neither here nor there,
but fast.
Place is being still.

AFTER PERRAULT
OR, IT'S NOT THE WITCH'S STORY

Left by oneself to oneself like the crone in the tower,
ask: Did she sleep with the sleepers? It never was clear.
Snow comes down on this breathing house and the hour
eats at the fire; the beer-cans they left on the floor
wink in the shadows like wetness on leaves.

    Suppose the morning: white on white
    descent of gulls on gull-colored snow.
    The given returns to whatever it is that gives
    (though which is which I hardly know)
    and gulls will come from wherever they spend the night
    to wherever it is they go.
    Suppose that wherever that is is here.
    Listen for breathers, asleep in their stories
    deeper drifted than drifts outside
    (the wind that nudges the house is wind, that's all:
    it is something else that shudders and hurries)
    Still in the spinning, where no snow falls,
    where the beast turns prince on the lips of the bride,
    is it one story only, or many—or none:
    the green quest dreamed in a winter dawn
    so white white gulls are grey beside?
    Ask, and suppose . . .

What reticence withheld just one detail
when every other circumstance was told?
The soldier lay unconscious in the keep;
cook by the cold hearth; shepherd in fold;
waiting ladies waited, loyal in sleep;
even a fading arras on the wall,
some little cups of never-tarnished gold
fallen among vines that sprung the sill:
all slept. But what of her that laid the spell?

I am concerned with spindles: did the crone
brew a poison to which she was immune?
Or are old women naturally prone
to touch with care what princesses disdain
to dread? The text they left us does not say
if she turned the point upon herself and slept
beside the girl, or sleepless spun away
a hundred years of sleep, a witch inept.

    Snow gives itself, unasked.
    Receiving is something else: a learned art
    of which the storyteller may have guessed
    enough to cut his spinner's story short.
    Feathered flesh descends from sky to water
    on errands of its own, given to self
    like showers of presents upon birthdays
    (unasked, unasked, my enchanted sleepers!
    all unasked, my king's daughter.)

Could not the gifted hag have charmed herself
and joined her princess when the web of creepers
caught the clock that last struck nine for twelve?
The thorns are blossoming a purple red
around their hearts tonight: if none have bled
it only signifies they have not stirred,
for dropping petals cover them, like blood.

At loss beside the cooling fire, I fear
the advent of the beast that bone to bone
will kiss them back to wakefulness: peer
of the realm who now is flayed, disguised, undone
(or do I mix my tales?) I cannot charm
him whole again nor predicate his changes
as waiting walls and towers are overgrown
—or even as the coal greys and falls.

The snow is pressing on the window sash
as if to keep my breathers inside warm
and I am locked in morning with the gulls
that call to other gulls across the hush,
contemporaneous with ends my strangers.

CYNICK SONNETS FOR THREE HOLYDAYS

(I) Good Friday AM, Without Cock-Crow

All innocent of chickens, zones of day's
Light comfort come to mitigate the dark.
The trailing habit of the morning greys
The edge of night's event without remark
From that all-but-anachronistic bird,
Now banned in suburbs and superfluous
On farms. Yet one may wake who never heard
Of lauds and matins gallinaceous,
To cold reflection that the crucial trial
Cannot find him at his level worst
Whose each installment of the Great Denial
Is paid ungrudgingly (beyond the first)—
    And words for which he'd face the martyr's pyre
    Served up with cocktails at a cook-out fire.

(II) All-Souls' in the Suburbs

A lighted porch awaits the rite forlorn
Of half-embarrassed children: time to fix
A votive treat of colored candy corn
(Though these familiars know few Stygian tricks).
This night the Beltane bonfires beckoned home
The fathers gone to dwell in druid dark
Not far outside. Here, quiet prowl-cars roam
Our leafless streets to regulate the lark
Of little spooks in sheets and solemn hats
To whom authentic spectres nod in vain—
Their sabbat cut-and-dried as paper cats
They pasted on the first-grade window pane.
    Who stands outside the door without disguise,
    Him only, one might fear to recognize.

(III) Advent on Route One

I drive a self-illuminated tunnel
Between the towns this latening night and year:
Municipally-metered Light Eternal
Stars a tree in every sleepy square.
Old Anthropologist, remember how
We climbed Your oaks to gather scraps of green
And hung them, like this fire-retarded bough,
To tell ourselves the year was young again?
The solstice turns on plastic-holly rope
Swung over shopping plazas: archetype
Of any business cycle's springing hope
That green may harvest gold when time is ripe.
    Then how astonishing, this civic crèche:
    Creator who would risk created flesh!

"Eppur si muove"
(For Jonathan Barker, on his birthday)

Dear Jonathan, your twenty years of living
I now salute, and quickly beg forgiving:
Your older relatives will light your cake
for themselves, as much as for your sake;
will count your candles as their own arrears,
measure in you the debt they owe the years.

A better ode, composed before the birth,
would have at least a documentary worth:
preserve that moment of neutrality
while born and unborn wait what is to be,
unseparated by the differential
of what for me is done, for you potential.
The poet sang the son of Pollio
(an eclogue written for an embryo)
all promise, prophecy, and golden scope:
for him who was, for him to be—a hope,
but you, two decades in the world, must hear
upon your birthday, "I remember, dear . . ."

How can an ancient aunt felicitate
a nephew born in nineteen thirty-eight?
Remembering your summer, how resist
the urge to tell you some of what you missed?
How have you understand, at least to pause
to think of how we thought we had a Cause?
When Spain was less a country on a chart
than the sensible dimension of the heart
we shook collection cans in subway trains.
(Then your mother had her labor pains)
When whimsy dates your dealings with the stork
the Ebro was a river in New York;

the stones and bones of Guernica were scattered
among illusions, similarly shattered;
we learned too late. How strange that you were there
but in your crib in Cambridge, couldn't care—
and even now, can hardly credit passion
that helped to put all Causes out of fashion.

No buttons now to wear, no funds to raise,
when to protest is merely not to praise,
and to be wisest is to seem the least,
to join the others in precarious feast
and snatch the comforts which the century
prepares to carry to eternity.
(For he will outwardly the best conform
himself the surest proof there is no norm.)

So, if your anniversary I sing
midsummer phantoms yet remembering,
the point will not be lost that we were such
as tried, but doubtless talked too much:
the answer easy and the slogan sure
of some who cared for what they couldn't cure.
Since you were later born, too old for these,
your hand may learn the lightning bolt to seize;
self-won, an older prophecy fulfill
that bids you bend creation to your will.

Thus, Jonathan, I celebrate your day
and on your table one more present lay:
the private hieroglyphic of my love—
in twenty years it moves; "The earth does move".

FRAGMENT

On an attic window sill
where the February sun
briefly warms it moves a fly,
only one:
roused to simulated summer
in a hollow time of frost,
memento of a world where flies
were lost,
all in one catastrophe
of last October—now
next spring's debris.

Having found unsought salvation
in this warmish winter hole,
does it like the fate that left it
safe, but sole?

MR. EWING, MR. DONN* AND THAT RAINBOW SIGN

Here is no age to bloom an August morning,
No era's dawning one might crane to witness
At late October twilight; we for whom
The prophets man a line of early warning,
Who concern ourselves about our fitness
And have made quite other plans for doom,
Find data on the water-level dull
(Although metastasis of tidal sloughs
Will be syndicated front-page news
The day that Boston's M.T.A. is full.)

A slap of waves will break the Arctic hush
To celebrate the freedom of the seas:
A hundred solid centuries
Gone soft, and no apocalyptic roar
To give us notice; only summer slush
Getting dirty under northern trees.

Next year, perhaps, we'd better try the shore;
For after these subsumed eternities
There won't be any rush,
And we can sit here some millennia more.
Not that we will let it catch us napping,
The neap-tides running underneath the door:
Oh, no.
As water pours across the Greenland sill
We will know it by its lapping
On our sea-walls long before
The night when it begins to spill
Down the cellar stairs, and we must go.

Time enough to think of moving when
Those snows (like old times, we will say at first)
Find summer neither long nor warm enough
And settle down upon the last moraine
To pack the stone-walled pastures with the stuff
Of glaciers. Then, too carefully rehearsed
In causes and too chilled for tears,
We'll leave, to seek New England's soil again
After exile—thirty thousand years.

There's little in the prospect to appall
A people used to mending wall;
Nor anything that we must now decide:
Nothing pressing, only to abide.
But much as I am loath to doubt the word
Of scientists who gauge the ocean's climb,
There's an older prophecy I've heard:
"It won't be water but be fire, next time."

*Two earth scientists who, in the International
Geophysical Year (1958) published the theory that
foresees a melt-down of the Arctic, a rise of the
sea-level, and an increase of precipitation that will,
in time (much time), bring back the glaciers that
once covered the land on which we live.

FIRST PERIOD

That day a door that hitherto stood wide
(Of its existence we were just aware)
Banged shut, surprising one of us outside.
We hushed, with half a thought we'd hear him there
Rattle the latch, indignant to get in,
But soft as chalk-dust in that vacancy
Misgiving settled, whether he had been
Excluded by the close event, or we.
The room was filled as fast as we could chatter:
Each told the other what each knew before,
For any fact about him seemed to matter
Now that it was clear there'd be no more.
      But what we mainly said remained unsaid,
      Such fine distinction comes of being dead.

BLOCK ISLAND, AGAIN

The numbered summers fuse to form a tense,
Past-present: separate identities
Abandoned on the beach, mere incidence
Of anglers come to plumb reflective seas.
Once more our changing shore affects no change:
The tufts of seedless grasses on its dunes,
Its wild rugosas, offer nothing strange
To twenty years of August afternoons.
The house, that quietly collects old shoes
And lobster-buoys, is like the sand around it:
Nothing important here to find or lose,
None to say for sure who lost or found it.
     A season's passenger, I scan the shore
     For children who picked up these shells before.

PRISONERS' BASE

Go down the after-dishes dark to find
that place the branches overhung the barn:
an oak-leaf eyrie with a roof for floor
the others never even knew was there.
Game after game, before whoever was *It*,
eyes equitably covered by his arm,
had counted out a hundred, you were set
to play—the hunted or the hunter, now one
now the other (O, they were not the same).

"Ready or not," *It* chanted. "here I come."

The way the Ozark man turns loose his hounds
and listens by his all-night fire, rejoices
or mourns to the music of the distant pack
(his study not their quarry but their voices)
you listened then, eyes shut against the black
enclosing leaves you knew were really green,
as one by one, their secret places found
(at times so near to yours you heard the trembling
of the hider's breath as *It* closed in)
the captives joined their captors. Assembling
without distinction then, they searched a while
together and gave up, one by one. Some spoke
of leaving you to rot, but raised the call.

Go find that place if it is there: dumb place
might tell, not why you roosted in the oak,
the spiderweb you feared across your face,
but rather why you joined the game at all:
and why, alone uncaught, why even then
you waited in your hot barked skin
and made the captive captors yell again
"All outs in free! Come in. Come in."

GRADE CROSSING, 1933

A small departure will elude excuse,
The implication of its vagrancy
Impugn the settlement of old abuse
That makes of larger vice good company.
Still returns an early freight train crawling
Through splendid ruined spring, and one who waved
While I stared out the seconds past recalling:
Too young, I tell myself, too well-behaved
To know the moment when to raise a hand
Is just a moment, given once, for then
The freight stretched out its length across the land
And there were other box-cars, other men.
    But one, upon that fresh regretted morning,
    Went un-sped, unscorned for all my scorning.

ADVICE TO A SELF-PORTRAIT

Here, but for that Garden incident
            (temptation's metaphor was born in want
            for fruit is precious in an arid land)
here might you be contained, almost content
to breathe the ample air, a standing man
who felt no need to move to find what space
he occupies or does not fill. But the paint
that put you on this ground so still
has all but covered up your face.

How is it I can see you only when
you move: now in the next field but one,
your not-unfriendly wave against the sky
whose larger motion makes a canvas still
enough to picture yours?
                        (The lizard is a stone
            until it breaks off basking on the wall;
            grasshopper grassblade unless it flies:
            if green takes fright, seeks food, it is not grass,
            though green. We do not speak of it the same.)
Your going leaves your figure undiminished:
only your work gains distance as you pass
beyond the pier and vaulting that you wished
and painted. What is picture now, what frame?

Here, for all that garden held, the man
like you might stand in space, nonchalant,
his feet grown plant-like in the ground.
       (We do not know if scissors hurt the rose;
       the trampled grass goes down without a sound;
       the sentient beast, it seems, does not lament
       his place nor seek in it such fruit that pain
       becomes the measure of the thing he knows.)
How is it, then, the garden has a fence
forbidding blank to him who stands outside,
yet separated all its breadth and length
by slits too narrow for the eye's wide
angle of vision to take the scene
within and make it whole? There is no gate.

Run, run! You will not see unless you run
an old Man and Woman breakfasting
among lilies where a bird-stained Pan
pipes beside a broken fountain; sun
warms the early apples on their plate;
their fingers touch as if the thought of love
had only just occurred to them this morning.
Two ancient statues, they appear to move
as under water: steriopticon
effect, perhaps . . . The motion is your own.

Run, standing man, run! There is no gate;
a world to move, there is no place to stand.
And while we talk of space and time and art
we nibble on the rosy fruit in spite
of what we guess is gnawing at its heart.

The Man and Woman only took a bite.

"... questa selva selvaggia ..."

Look back once more to see if you can see
        the road (was there a road?) by which we came
        to stand beneath this unfamiliar tree.

The frantic shadows dance along the same
        as those that beckoned us an hour ago:
        here is a signpost, but it bears no name.

We walk too fast. Or do we go too slow?
        We've barely made our way into the wood,
        yet see the wilderness behind us grow!

Might we go back to stand where once we stood
        and find ourselves still waiting in the clearing?
        —A vine with thorns like little drops of blood

has grown around us front and back obscuring
        the path that anciently another made,
        the twilight of no less a doubt enduring.

Look back. Look down into the darkening glade:
        a shadow among shadows. Is it he?
        And will you ask directions of a shade?

TO COLUMBIA UNIVERSITY, RIVERSIDE CHURCH, ET AL.
(Upon the Twentieth Anniversary of their
"Slum Clearance" Project)

Nine-headed Hypocrite upon the Hill
Whose multi-million-dollar Belgian chimes
Have quartered all the hours since the times
That you, no less than we, remember still,
Do you feel safer since you've worked your will?
Your neighbor has departed, and his crimes;
The grandson of the Old Man of the Dimes
His function did, in spite of us, fulfill.
Now Harlem's households, cleared by Title One,
Are no more visible from Morningside
And fourteen stories of expensive stone
Veil other vistas you prefer to hide:
    "No place to go", to which we now are gone,
    Whose play of color you could not abide.

DEMOLITION DIRGE

Walk with me our street, unbidden,
For you carry now no key;
See the gorgeous new-made midden
Where the houses used to be:
Visible the one-time hidden
Haunts of pastel privacy.
The swinging ball
Claims all.

Under scaffolding of shutters
Faced with pink and yellow doors,
Name the numbers no one utters
Since they lost their upper floors:
Ghosts in summer-running gutters
Where a trash-remover roars.
The swinging ball
is taking all . . .

All the staid, old-fashioned houses
Lined with Puerto Rican paint
(The Authority espouses
A decor of more restraint:
What its Housing Law allows is
Free of Caribbean taint.)
The swinging ball
Exposes all

Here, among remembered flowers
Of a land we'd never seen
We beguiled an age with hours
Not exactly gold, but green:
Now a clamshell bucket towers
Over that fragmented scene.
The swinging ball
Has done, withal.

Did we nothing leave behind us
To assert our presence there,
So a neighbor still might find us
If he came and looked with care?
Or did that which seemed to bind us
Go like plaster in the air?
The swinging ball
Leaves no recall.

When the project houses follow
These into the cellar-holes,
And their bricks have filled a hollow
Of those artificial shoals
Where the party-boats now wallow
Furred both sides with fishing poles,
Will the ball
Still fall?

Pulverize progressive plunder,
Tuck it in some kelpy rift?
Expeditions, lost in wonder,
Ages hence may dig and sift
For a broken cup of under-
standing in the dateless drift:
The ball
Will leave it small.

Leveled Troy was not so cryptic
And the potsherds of Bath-Shan
Left a message less elliptic
Than our tidy colophon:
Here, no glyph of mural lipstick
Will record that Jane loved Juan.
The swinging ball
Is all.

LETTER FROM MRS. HOSHINO

That garden in Manhattanville
    we tended every year until
    they tore the houses down to clear the slums:
    now who comes?
The hyacinth is starred
    and every twinkling shard
    of bottle-glass that lies among the weeds
    an amaranthine garden seeds
    for growth that neither blooms nor fades.

"What happened to the children with the spades?"

In Eden after Babel, these
    never needed apple trees:
    for none would clear the innocence
    of any kid who climbed the fence,
    polychrome and polyglot,
    to plant that lot.
Now a last-week's green-sheet blows
and candy wrappers gather 'round the rose,
almost as gay.

"The children with the spades have moved away?"

Bulbs they planted back in fifty-one
    respond to April's touch, all diggers gone
    these several years;
    in the corner volunteers
    of johnny jump-up still declare
that someone planted there.
Yet another crop now thrives . . .

"even in the twenty-story hives?"

but no one stands beside the gate to call
them in from playing ball:
to seed the soil and greet the sprout
and learn what harvest's all about,
the way they did it in those days
before the urban clearance craze
sent child and parent from that place,
fallen from grace.

"Resolve me of all ambiguities"
(Quiz-Show "Twenty-One," in November, 1959:
the Van Doren scandal)

Contracting time that nurtured his researches
Now squeezes tears he hitherto contained:
What harm with grapes to please a pregnant duchess
Or that an emperor was entertained?
The thing was legal, save that little matter
Of forty dollars for a horse, dissolved:
The buyer sought and found his own deep water;
The Doctor, strictly speaking, is absolved.

Of all the trite astronomy that whirled
Him into fame, one answer (never given)
"Sweet Mephistophilis, Who made the World?"
Might even late have let him try for Heaven.

A closing scenic thunder drowns all thought of it:
Why, this is the hour. Nor am I out of it.

ART, LIFE, AND A HIRSCHKÄFER

Albrecht Dürer drew
  a beautiful stag-beetle in battle attitude
  in fifteen-five.
Now, in proper season I could catch a bug for you
  whose verisimilitude
  would be even more masterly in view
  of the fact that it would also be alive.
  But who wants to?
Dürer's model is undeniably dead
  and so is he
  who, on occasion, is said to have said
  that God gives such a hand as his only once or twice
  a generation,
  which, though true, did not suffice
  for immortality
  that Dürer in person (it would seem) found satisfying
Since Creation
the good artists, the mediocre, and the poor ones
are all dead or dying
and beetles return with every summer's grass
without Dürers:
  by June the burnished exoskeletons
  arm a procreative rage;
  on file-like feet they pass,
  fierce gesturers
  with razored mandibles erect
  and ready to engage
  in the manner of the Reformation insect.

Were I an entymologist I might
view this angry lustre in another light,
but as things stand
the point about the beetle in respect
to beetleness, for me,
is what another eye could see
and the purpose that informed a once-a-generation hand
early in the sixteenth century.

At least, so I opined
until one buzzed my bedroom, flying blind.

IN THE OLD CENTER CEMETERY, ROXBURY, CT

The briefer children of the town
in ranks around their parents lie,
whose stones, illegible and brown,
among the nettles lean awry.

"Be fruitful," said the Lord, "and multiply."

A churchless churchyard, filled and left
behind in an unpastured field:
these young bereavers, old bereft,
the eighteenth century congealed.

Listen. Nothing here is still
except the mould beneath the mounds:
a tractor works on Tophet Hill;
the highway hums its background sounds;
the air brings news of distant drilling;
and insects, omnipresent, lost
in grass, their cycle's phase fulfilling,
count down the borrowed days till frost.

"How sad" (I wave away the bugs)
"How sad," I say, "each little grave."
"Thank God," you say, "for wonder drugs
"and all the parents' tears they save."
"Here, (I peer) Josiah Baker,
"his wife and latest daughter lie:
"'God, who gave, was soon to take her.'
"Ten were born, with six to die."

"Be fruitful," said the Lord, "and multiply."

(Some say it will not take a bomb
to make our planet home a tomb,
but simply love and sanitation
will bring the final desolation:
when all whom death has not undone
beneath a simultaneous sun
emerging in warm floods of birth
will chew the surface off the earth.
Already now, the vague unease—
so many Indians and Chinese.)

"The little mounds," I say, "How sad,
"and yet . . . with over-population . . ."
"Thank God," you say, "our own have had
"the latest in inoculation!"

Born down by seed, the grasses bend;
a swallow scoops along the sky;
a cricket senses summer's end
and gives his tedious little cry.

"Be fruitful," said the Lord, "and multiply."

A DRY DEFINING

Of all the awaited water that after
such drought ought to come
(so we told God)
only drops fell, fat and few,
soon gone, though thunder-heads
all afternoon hung over pastures:
hay uncut (not worth the cutting)
bending under something running
home before the storm.

But not that day
nor weeks of days thereafter
came anything but piled clouds:
sun now shrouded now uncovered,
precipitation promised and withdrawn,
while over the long-distance phone
the movers and the shakers weighed
the definition of a word.

Some suggested that we pray
for rain or more distinct "disaster," one:
petition God or government,
empyrean or Washington,
to end the drought or make it pay.

Intercession crawled at length
along the roads, ruinous,
in trailer-truckloads of Canadian hay.

THE MUSE MOVES TO NEWTON

Call not the field mouse or the mole
Poisoned in his earthy hole,
But watch the evening traffic pass
And cut the grass.

Plant your garden at the rear
Where nothing of it will appear,
Hyacinths and laurel trees
That no one sees.

There a wilderness immure
to wander, safely insecure,
But weave the wall about it thrice
And keep the front yard looking nice.

If a distant horn is blowing,
This time you will not be going,
Not be running to inquire
"Where's the fire?"

Better trim the walk and wait
Than tempt the patience of the Fate,
For under these enameled lawns
Avernus yawns.

Relaxing on the grassy verge
Begin, Sicilian Muse, your dirge:
The instantaneous relief
Of merely private grief.

FOR TWO VOICES AND A HALF-BUILT BRIDGE

The bridge
half flung over the water
gorgeous in iron-oxide paint and evening sun said
"I am not broken, not the Pont d'Avignon,
but a new bridge almost done."

Had it not been for that
and the bewildering barricades
warnings
the gathering of silent but sociable
brontosauri staked out for the night:
in short, had the detour held fewer associations
Jurassic and otherwise
I would not have missed the highway
and taken this road to the ocean.

"It isn't a serious mistake.
We have plenty of time."

Do you think you are expected
or are expecting something?
If this blacktop ends at a lobsterman's shack
with late September marigolds among the traps
then this is That Road . . . .

The transformation is considerable
but is it significant?
The shack,
two hurricanes and a lobster syndicate ago,
has yielded to fried clams, closed.
New cottages
boarded since school opened and mindful of the equinox,
stand on precautious stilts over the salt hay:
incidental details.

"Will God back-date the Judgment Day
to make us feel at home?
dissolve the new developments with Trump of Doom;
re-form
the Rhode Island shore of nineteen-forty, say?"

The inlet purples under shadows from the shore
this hour, this season, nineteen years ago;
but this ocean is not the one we saw before.

By myself I only guess at
who was here.
Landscape with figures: double negative
caught,
twice exposed and a little out of register,
we pose in Heracleitan trance:
"What if they left that bridge as is,
to use for dancing—
the military and the Capucins?"

"What if?"
Those two were we.
"What if" is what we then embraced and wed:
demanded not
to have, to do, but simply be,
to make it possible to find again
again again
the old familiar strange:
each, together, self-possessed, possessing
one beloved shape of human change.

DEED

Lawyers kill me
with their antique diction,
bounded and butted as the bounds and butts now stand,
their cloth-taped, blue-foldered fiction
that anybody anywhere owns land.

Here, in spite of
their best intentions,
they manage not to mention almost everything:
include the meadow but not the gentians,
the spring but not the frog in the spring;
and nothing about old lilac hedges
or hands by which they must have been planted,
or are these
the appurtenances, rights, and privileges
(like brown pear trees)
hereby sold, conveyed, and granted?

Beginning where
now stands, or formerly stood . . .
running westerly along a stone wall . . .
(The old barn rotted in the wood:
its builder doesn't run at all.)
Lawfully seized
in fee simple (simple, indeed!)
The thicket is bounded, but what of its pheasants?
What of the root, and the seed?
the farmer, and the farmer's boy?
At all times hereafter, know by these presents . . .
quietly, peaceably, have and enjoy.

No man
was by covenant ever so blest
since Adam his orchard was thinning,
and his heirs and assigns
were seized and possessed
of their lot and its lines
(like this lot and its lines)
running East North and West:
thence South, to the place of beginning.

RONDEAU FOR ANNUALS IN OCTOBER

As flowers fall to feed the blaze
that fast consumes these dwindling days,
in common cause with kindling weed
the seedling bears in living seed
the stigma of its dying phase.

Escaping in mid-autumn's haze,
a garden someone worked to raise
makes doer stranger to the deed
as flowers fall.

The tilting hemisphere arrays
these teeming files where each obeys
the prompting of its pollened breed
in sanguine petals where I read
non nobis, nobis. How else praise
the flowers' fall?

TWENTY DAYS, TWENTY YEARS
(Aubade and Berceuse for a Son)

I

Wake, my child,
the Peaceable Kingdom
sits in twos upon the lawn:
long ago and soon in one,
the time that it is once upon,
lamb and vegetarian lion.
Wake up, love, and bid them come.

End your sleep.
The innocent breath
that hangs above you like a wraith
is what your father called them with
who spoke the only tongue on earth
when language had no word for death.
Up, new-born, command a birth!

Open your eyes:
they wait for you,
gentle and curious, damp with dew;
but hawk will rise when day turns blue
and hound and mourning-dove will go
where you might ask a lifetime through.
Wake, and remember the words you knew.

II

Could I say, "Your question bores the Fates,"
since golden boughs occur in any wood
and fathers are by definition wrong
on evils that are bred of too much good?
Or play for time: "The Sibyl meditates"?

You will be miserable, but not for long:
attention wanders as an answer waits.

Eye wanders to the pattern on the plates;
hand creeps to hand beside yours under the table;
ear hears the words but strains to catch the song
that has no words. Meanwhile the Oracle,
familiar with the young, procrastinates.

You will be miserable, but not for long:
attention wanders as an answer waits.

Could I say, "Perhaps it is the same
thing in the end if you have stood
outside the temple listening to the gong
count down—or cooled your sacrificial blood
in bed? The Sibyl some time learns your name.

If you were miserable, it was not long.
for sleep had come before an answer came.

IDENTITY, IN BLACK AND WHITE
(For Benny)

Staring down long ancestors
in the late night's mirror
(the bathroom bulb gone out again)
the face I took to work this afternoon
is locked behind the shadowed glass like some
dim photo that I knew another time:
yellowed grandfather, younger than I am
on the plastic pass that's pinned secure
inside my coat. (It shows that I was cleared.)
Who looks like this at me?
(The gateman hardly glances up; he knows
I never was a risk—and I am cleared.)

Back downtown before the Palace closes,
cornered with coffee later than I'd planned
(Where did I see that picture hung, what room?)
the conversation stirs around to fathers:
I sit it out; the answer has no question.
(I wonder can I sleep if I go home)

What put him in the mirror? No one
ever said I looked like him, but he
(never had his picture made but once,
his wedding day, I'll bet)
—he must have looked like me
(to think of it, he didn't need that one,
never having had to pass a gate
between the house and where the work was done,
except to keep the hogs and chickens in.)

His eyes hold onto mine: his mouth,
something like a smile or like a scar,
says nothing I can hear
(Heart pumps loud at night: by day
you don't remember it is there.)

What happened to the photo of his wife?
And his father, and his father's father?
Back and back they go till here am I,
like the picture on the Old Dutch Cleanser
of the picture on the Old Dutch Cleanser
(a can I used to call infinity)
or like to tell the truth I say I lie
or like you've got to love yourself to love another.

You turn, and find you're on another corner;
you get your clearance, but the risk
has ways of waiting for you in the mirror
(*He* took it or he'd not have come as far
as me, is all I know. I wish he'd answer
but I don't know what it is I want to ask.)

I think of his dark house and wonder
how he made it, and his father and his father,
how they stood it in the shadow and the light.
Or did the cow, bellowing her full udder,
the fire to feed, the bottomland to plow
leave too little time for riddling mirrors?
(Maybe there were no mirrors)

My nightshift refuge from the night
must do for now.

MNEMOSYNE GERIATRICE

You, Memory, are like my aging hound
who often doesn't hear me when I whistle
but pricks her ears at the remotest sound,
reacting with a wag, a whine, a bristle.

So often, Muse, I hail you to the phone
to ask you what I heard there yesterday,
but find that you are tripping off alone,
summoned by some voice from far away—

a voice of ancient accent, hard to hear
above the racket of the century,
yet one that makes us wonder if this year
will open up that door called "destiny."

We're out of fashion now, to be harassed
by riddles of apocalyptic risk:
the present generation puts its past
and future on the hard computer disk.

THE TRADITION STILL TRADUCES

In Medfield, Massachusetts,
in a place named Norfolk now,
King Philip's fellows put some people
in a line of little graves
around a road-bend from the Big One.

Now geese and gulls, whose forebears saw
the Great Swamp Fight and Philip's fall,
wing over walls strung out along
the wetlands won by those who drove
the Dragon to his Mount Hope den.
It proved the "prison" where he met
"God's Messengers of Death," avengers
of those pious pioneers
tucked away before their time
by the Medfield "massacre"—word
that named an Indian victory
as "battle" did an English one.

I walk these wetlands now and wonder
if the world we take and make with words—
words like "massacre" or "battle,"
"crime" or "war"—is not the same
as that old howling wilderness
where once New England's new Isaiah
named the natives "Evening Wolves,"
called them God's new "Rod of Anger"
(not Assyrians now, but animals)
"Generations of the Dragon,"
"Python," Typhon," and "'Leviathan":
monsters out of myth and Bible
all designed by the Divine One
to keep New Israel in line,
press His backslid Puritans
to beat the beast in each man's breast,
seek and slay it in the forest
in war upon its Indian metaphor

So they solved it, those old settlers
of these one-time savage suburbs—
dressed sin in feathers and red skin,
grabbed the ground and saved their souls
and taught us how to do it:
Turn your problems into demons,
your temptations into Typhons,
fears to Furies, doubts to devils,
evil thoughts to enemies.
Exorcise them! Find your fiend
in the body of the other,
in the victim's guilty color,
in the anger of the alien.
Turn familiars into strangers,
creatures of another species
you can cause to disappear
and, without regret, forget.

Now, like monuments to men
who cleared their consciences in clearing
Mather's monsters off this land,
long prison walls surround our sins,
enclose our errors, hide our hang-ups,
in the fields their fight bequeathed us
beside old Medfield cemetery
with old King Philip's Trail nearby,
now so tame and orderly:
the forest gone, and native animals—
save seagulls gobbling prison garbage,
protected geese in honking passage,
projected evils locked inside
to keep ourselves by self unseen.
The wilderness has never died,
it seems, but only gone within.

GRAND GRANDCHILD

Gia Barker, twenty years
living like a lively leaven
in the dough of these dumb times,
I start to greet your day with cheers
but think of nineteen-sixty-seven
bedeviled by three other rhymes,
plagued by jeers and tears and fears—
a grandma born nineteen-eleven,
caught in clashing paradigms.

The year you came, the marching songs
of those who warred against the war
were sounding hope your time would see
a righting of those ruling wrongs
my bunch had battled years before—
but learned to live with, comfortably.
Small wonder you are one who longs
to end the bedlam, break the bore
we willed to our posterity!

The hope returns with ones like you
who wish the world to help renew.
Today I celebrate your birth
as happy birthday for the earth!

Elizabeth Jackson Barker, born in northern Michigan in 1911, came from families whose ancestors included underground-railroad Quakers of eastern Pennsylvania and a Mohawk chieftain of upstate New York. (Her first poem, at age seven, extolled Indians.) After childhood and adolescence in several midwestern states (mainly Missouri), she went to Stanford University in California where she studied history until, in 1934, she married Guy Barker. For most of their fifty-four years together they lived in New York, Connecticut and Massachusetts, where they engaged in various social causes, worked for map and model makers, raised three children, tilled the soil, and earned graduate degrees in literature and philosophy (at Trinity College in Hartford).

Guy Barker became an inventive furniture designer; Elizabeth an associate professor (now emeritus) of English and Liberal Studies at Boston University, where, with Guy's help and advice, she ran (and stills runs) a degree program for prisoners. While poetry was her first love and a lasting one, the issues of the era, plus the fascination of teaching B.U.'s students both on campus and in the prisons—where a liberal arts education produces new perspectives on the world—took precedence over a career of writing and publishing. She continues, however, to sponsor poetry readings by prisoners. She publishes now primarily to honor the memory of her recently-deceased husband, Guy Barker, who was her primary inspiration.